ELVIRA

*A Woman of
Strong Faith in God*

RUBY MILLS

First published in Australia 2019
This edition published 2019
Copyright © Ruby Mills 2019
Cover design, typesetting: Working Type Studio, Melbourne

The right of Ruby Mills to be identified as the Author of the Work has been asserted in accordance with the Copyright, Designs and Patents Act 1988.

All rights reserved. No part of this publication may be reproduced, stored in a retrieval system, or transmitted, in any form or by any means without the prior written permission of the publisher, nor be otherwise circulated in any form of binding or cover other than that in which it is published and without a similar condition being imposed on the subsequent purchaser.

Mills, Ruby
Elvira: A Woman of Strong Faith in God
ISBN (pbk): 978-0-6485893-8-9
pp116

ACKNOWLEDGEMENTS

My sincere thanks to Lorna Ramirez, for helping me to pursue my dream of having my autobiography. Without her, publishing my life's story in a book would not be a possibility.

ABOUT THE AUTHOR

Elvira Ramirez Rostata was born in the Philippines at Caibiran Leyte on the 21st of November 1962.

At an early age she had endured many trials and tribulations, thus making her a stronger person and with a sheer determination to succeed in life.

She managed to own a small business in food in Pampanga, Philippines where she met her soulmate Barry Mills, a tourist from Australia. They were married on the 12th of August 1985 at the Church of Christ in Angeles City Pampanga. After a year, on March 11, 1986 she migrated to Australia to be reunited with her beloved husband Barry Mills. They were blessed with three wonderful sons, but unfortunately her husband Barry died in 2018.

Elvira loves to interact with people and her present job as a carer in one of the nursing homes in Victoria gives her the opportunity to help, and serve the elderly. She is now living life to the fullest and her happiest moments will be, when she is surrounded with family and friends.

THIS BOOK IS DEDICATED TO:

My husband Barry Mills who passed away 2018
My children Darren Mills, David Mills, and Grant Mills

CONTENTS

ACKNOWLEDGEMENTS III
THIS BOOK IS DEDICATED TO: V
CONTENTS VII
PREFACE 1
INTRODUCTION 3
CHAPTER 1:   MY FAMILY TREE 9
CHAPTER 2:   CHILDHOOD MEMORIES 13
CHAPTER 3:   GREENHILLS, SAN JUAN MANILA ... 27
CHAPTER 4:   ACTING CAREER 35
CHAPTER 5:   BINONDO MANILA 39
CHAPTER 6:   PAMPANGA 45
CHAPTER 7:   MY SOULMATE 51
CHAPTER 8: AUSTRALIA 59
CHAPTER 9:   MY HUSBAND BARRY MILLS 67
CHAPTER 10: LIFE WITHOUT BARRY 73
CHAPTER 11: MIRACLES 77
CHAPTER 12: FAMILY PHOTOS 89

PREFACE

Based on my life's story, this book was written so I may have a legacy to leave to my children and my future generations, hence they could know the story of their roots and where they came from. In this book I will be able to show them and teach the rich heritage of the Filipino culture and family values. In this book my children will be able to appreciate, the sacrifices I had endured in order to give them a better life in Australia.

INTRODUCTION

Caibiran is the province of the Eastern Visayas in the Philippines. It is the easternmost province of the Biliran Island and is situated beside the bay. My Name is Elvira Ramirez Rostata and I was born in the town of Caibiran Leyte on the 21st of November 1962. I am proud of my hometown and its rich in mineral resources. My town is surrounded by the Tinago, Caibiran, Manlabang, and Tumalists rivers, hence pressing an ever-looming threat of flooding especially during the rainy season. However, in the surrounding rivers are in

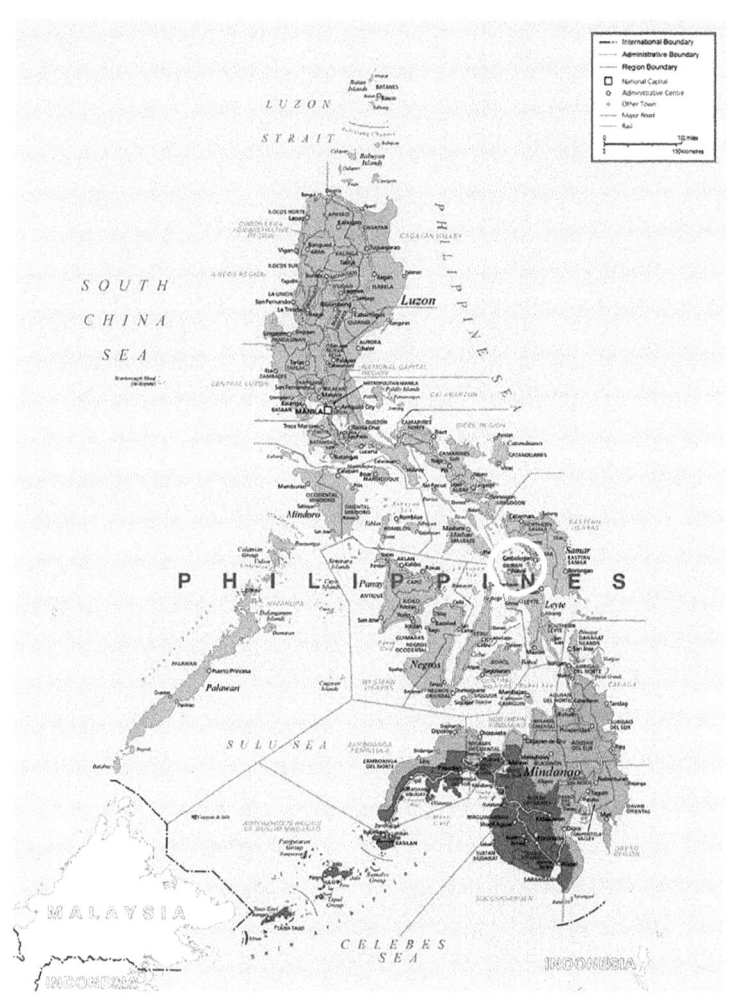

Philippines

INTRODUCTION

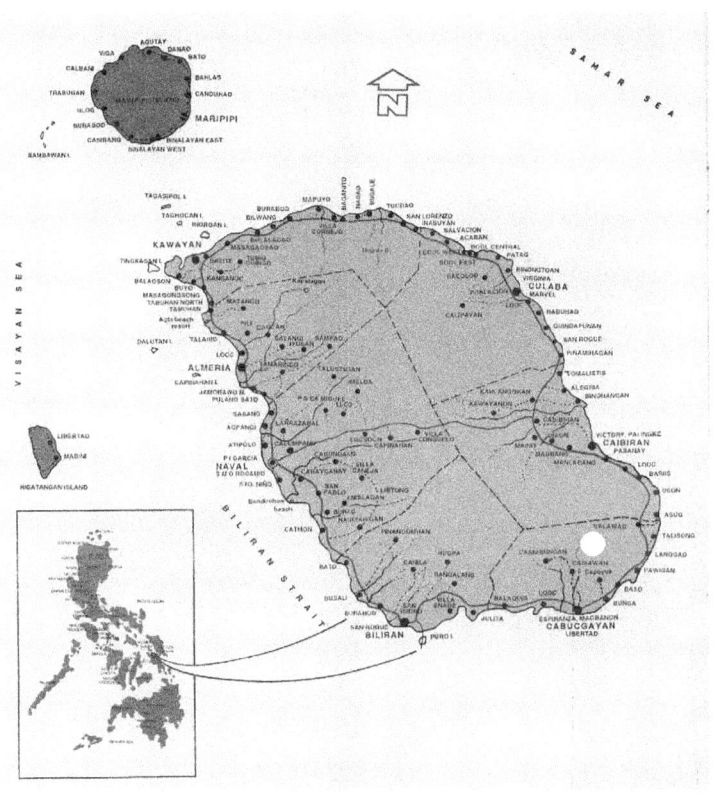

Biliran Island

abundance of fish, and Lizards called Ibid. This town is the main supplier of agricultural products to Tacloban, the highly urbanised city which neighbours ours. My Town has a hot spring that is Famous for its medicinal value.

CHAPTER 1:
MY FAMILY TREE

My mother's name is Maria Ramirez and my father was Lorenzo Rostata. I am the seventh of twelve siblings, having six brothers and five sisters. My brothers are Lamberto, Domingo, Antonio, Patricind Joselito, and my sisters, Norma, Lilia, Narcisa, Ramona, and Cirila. We are a big happy family.

We lived in a barrio and far from the city, so there was no hospital around the area. My mother gave birth to all of us at home with the help of a Hilot (a lady who practises massaging) as a token of appreciation we only gave the Hilot lady chicken and tobacco as form of payments. There were no midwives nor professional people to help us. Out of my siblings which were all born at home were born healthy and survived, except for one sibling. All of my brothers and sisters took care of my mom until she was back on her feet. For a month we gave mom concoction of medicinal roots and herbs to prevent infection.

My parents owned rice fields and big acre of land, producing coconut, and fruits and vegetables. Mum was interested in doing business by buying and selling of jewellery. She was also a good cook and often provided catering for the prominent people in our barrio for celebrations and fiesta in our town. Don Pedro Ramirez is the father of my mum. He was known, loved and respected in our barrio because of his generosity and kindness.

No matter what you are
No matter where you are
Do not forget your roots
Where you came from
Always cherish them in your heart
Thank those people who helped you
Of what you are today

By Lorna Ramirez

CHAPTER 2:
CHILDHOOD MEMORIES

The house that I grew up in in Caibiran was large and had a Spanish style and structure. Antique wood carvings were seen all over the house. The curves of the wooden fixtures were instantly noticeable on all the furniture such as the tables, chairs, and beds, which gave a European impression. The house had seven bedrooms spacious enough for all my siblings. Our house was surrounded with fruit trees; mangoes, avocado, lanzones, and many more. A heavenly luscious experience for fruit lovers. In our farm we have chicken, pig, cows and horses. We also had kalabaw (water buffalo) that my father used for farming. However, because we were surrounded by rivers, flooding is our main concern and to all people living in this barrio (district of a city town).

At the top of the mountain of Caibiran, we had a small bamboo house. From the top you can see and admire the whole city of Leyte. It is truly a magnificent view. The city view triggers my happy memories of going to the city. My mum knew that my heart desires to live in the big city and so she said, "Do not worry dear, your dream will come true one day." I looked at her and said, "Thanks mum I can do it".

At night, and especially during full moon, my grandparents (lola and lolo) would sit on the veranda and watch us play, the siblings and cousins. We played hide and seek, and a Spanish game called Patintero. In this game there are two teams, played with around six players or more. We would draw a rectangular grid on the ground, usually five to six meters long and three meters wide. One team are the taggers and the other team are runners. We decided who will play as taggers and runners by "Jak-en-poy" (rock-paper-scissors). The runners have to cross the rectangle grid without being tagged. It was really a fun game for us to play, and looking back now I have so many memories of playing in the dark, lit by dozens of Alitaptap (fireflies) that twinkle like stars and brighten the night. These memories from my childhood will always be in my heart to be cherished forever. Happiness during my childhood bonding with my families and friends will always be remembered.

The crystal water hot spring is just only few kilometres from our family home, and my mum often took us there for us to bathe and picnic, and at the same time she will wash our dirty linens and clothing. I spent the rest of the afternoon playing with my brothers and sisters.

When I was five years old, a storm hit our barrio. My father was in the rice field while I was asleep in the house, before being suddenly awaken by a strong pushing gush of wind. Water was rushing in to my house, quickly flooding the rooms. luckily mum came to find me, and with my baby brother in her arms she pulled and dragged me to safety. The current and the wind were so strong that our coconuts and other fruits were falling from the trees and nearly hitting us while we tried our best to evacuate and go to our Grandparents house. The rest of my brothers and sisters were already at my Grandparents place when we finally got there. My Grandparents house was a double story; high in structure and safe from the water.

After the flooding, we started planting new rice again and with good weather after six months we had an abundance of rice for harvest. This called for celebration to God and the Holy Spirit for the blessings. We had plenty of amazing food, and we sang and danced for the whole night. I had fun with my siblings and cousins for this celebration.

Fishing with my Dad when I was young was a very memorable experience. The rivers surrounding the Caibiran were so bountiful with fish that it was easy to catch them. They tasted so delicious when cooked and were enjoyed by the whole family. My Dad was also fond of hunting wild pigs which we then cooked as Lechon, a traditional Pilipino dish. The whole pig is cooked slowly over charcoal and rotated by hand on a bamboo spit.

Being the seventh sibling in the family I witnessed my mum giving birth each year for a few years. We were actually a family of twelve, but my younger brother died at the tender age of one. Though we are not rich, my parents worked hard so we always had food on our table, and we were a very grateful and tightly knoted family indeed.

Harana (serenade) is part of a tradition in the Philippines, especially in barrios, where the would-be-suitor will sing outside near the window of the lady he is courting. Together with him, his friends would back him up with guitar music and vocals. The young lass would then open the window to invite the young man and his friends into the house. The father and the daughter would be in the living room to greet the serenaders, and the father would ask questions about the suitor's family background, and his intentions with his daughter. My Ate (an address given to older sister) was often serenaded from aspiring suitors in our barrio. This tradition is seldom practice now in the Philippines.

The lower part of our house was full of coconut husks, and one night after a harana when we had all gone to bed my Father was woken up by our cat who jumped onto his chest in alarm. The husks under the house had started to ignite, possibly from a cigarette thrown by the people who had serenaded my sister that night. Fortunately, the fire was immediately put out before any damage was done.

At age nine, my siblings and cousins would often go to play at the large river nearby. We would bring along a lot of fresh fruits and food for our picnic for the day. As a kid I was embarrassed when my school crush passed by as I was naked and ready for a swim. I remember running in to the water so he wouldn't see me.

Another time at the river my cousin played a practical joke on me. He pushed and pulled me to the deepest part of the river and I didn't really know how to swim properly. He left me there and walked away while I was screaming and calling for help. I was really struggling and in my mind I was prepared to die. Thankfully luck was still on my side when a fisherman passed by and helped me. They pulled me out in the water, hence saving me from drowning. I developed a phobia of swimming in the open water which still haunts me to this day.

Our grandparents house was quite far from where we live. One day with my two-year-old sibling I decided to go to our grandparent's place without the consent or knowledge of my parents and older brothers and sisters. I loved going to my grandparents' house, they always cooked me paksiw na isda (fish with vinegar, slowly cooked in a terracotta pot) and jackfruit in coconut juice, boiled cassava, corn, or banana. Since it was getting late, my grandparents decided that we had to stay overnight at their place. At that time there was no telephone or mobile phone, nor any form of instant communication. My family were all so worried and I knew I was going to be in a big trouble when I got home. The following morning I had a good spanking from my older brother.

There was a time in my younger years where there was continuous rainfall. It flooded our rice fields so we had no choice but to search for some edible parts from the rice Field. While I was out looking, I stepped in to a patch of quick sand. My mother was close by and strong enough to pull me out before I would be submerged.

Having a big family of twelve children, my parents had the problem of feeding and supporting us especially when there were typhoons and floods that greatly affected our harvest and income. Although my father loved all his children, he was slowly becoming an alcoholic. He would do a headcount every night to make sure all the children were in the house. My elder brother who was already a teenager did not came home one night. He slept at the house of a friend. He had a good belting from my father. My father was strict, disciplinarian but he loved us with all his heart. We all grew up to be responsible adults.

Wedding celebrations were a whole barrio affair in the Philippines. When my sister got married in Leyte there was a huge celebration that lasted three days and three nights. She was so beautiful at her wedding, and her husband is from a prominent family in our barrio. We butchered two cows, water buffalo, wild pigs, and hundreds of chickens. Even those not invited came for the feast and celebration. Almost the whole barrio came to attend the wedding. Up to this present day I have not witnessed another wedding like this.

One memorable experience from when I was young was when we had a very strong typhoon destroy all our plantations and rice fields. We had nothing to eat so my dad decided to go to the field to gather the remaining sweet potato. On his way to home he said that he fell in the river and was only barely able to grab onto the edge of a big tree trunk. We waited for him until it was nearly midnight with still no sign of my father. We all thought that he wouldn't make it home. We all prayed hard for a miracle.

Then after about another hour of endless waiting,

we heard knocking on the door. It was my father, tired and looking weary. My mum asked how he managed to find the house since it was so dark during the night. My dad said between gasping sobs that he followed a light on the top of a house nearby that lead him towards our house. It was a miracle we all said.

All my family kneeled down and prayed again thanking God for his gift of a miracle.

There are memories
That are so priceless
To be forgotten
Especially memories of your childhood
That will always bring a smile
On your face, moments
Deeply treasured in your heart

By Lorna Ramirez

CHAPTER 3: GREENHILLS, SAN JUAN MANILA

There were too many typhoons and floods in our barrio; hence my mum made a decision to go to Manila to seek greener pastures. She stayed at her cousin's house in Greenhills, San Juan Manila. Greenhills is a first class highly urbanised city in metro Manila. It lies between Quezon City on its north and east and Mandaluyong on its south.

Lydia Ramirez is the name of my mum's cousin. She was very affluent, rich, and a prominent member of the community. They owned a mansion, with nine servants, and two chauffeurs. The house was picturesque, surrounded with beautiful stunning orchids. It was a posh neighbourhood. Prominent politicians, and famous actors and actresses with the likes of Nora Aunor, Josephine Estrada, Victor wood, Fernando Poe junior living there.

After few years of my mum staying at Greenhills she brought myself, my brother, and Ate Narcisa, to Manila to live with her and my auntie's family. I was ten years old at the time.

It felt like paradise living at my auntie Lydia's place. I felt safe, they were so nice and really looked after us, and I was treated as part of their close family. On Sunday mornings when we went to mass I would always see my favourite screen actors and actresses. It was amazing. At one stage my auntie wanted to adopt me and become my legal guardian, but both my mum and I declined the offer.

I was really over the moon when I was accepted at a public school in Manila. Having lived and grew up in a Visayan region, I had to adapt to the new environment. I studied hard and I became a teacher's pet. I would even help my teacher check the test papers. For the first time in my life my classmates started calling me names. I had never been bullied before this. There was one scenario when I was writing on the blackboard my classmate, a boy, threw a bunot at me (a half coconut husk used for cleaning wooden floors in the Philippines) and hit me on the back hard. I was so angry that I grabbed him, tore his shirt, and grabbed at his hair. He hurriedly went home and came back with his mother. I explained to the mother what happened and thankfully the mum understood my side and even apologised to me for what her son had done.

Even though we had everything at my auntie's place, my mum became restless and wanted her freedom. My mum is a strong minded person and she felt like she couldn't do what she wanted when staying in someone else's home, so she decided to leave Greenhills, much to the disappointment of my auntie. I remember my auntie saying, "Are you sure you can manage on your own?" and without hesitation my mum had replied, "Thanks for everything, for all the support your family had given us, but I want to spread my wings and this is what we want." With tears in our eyes my siblings and I said goodbye to our kind and beautiful auntie Lydia Ramirez.

CHANGE

Everything will come to an end
What was relevant before
Does not exist anymore
There will come a time that you want change
It's time to embrace a new chapter
In your life
This will be a new beginning
A new life and a new hope

By Lorna Ramirez

CHAPTER 4: ACTING CAREER

When I turned 18 years old, I tried my luck on the movie screen by playing as an extra or in supporting roles. I worked with famous thespians with the likes of Lorna Tolentino. Alma Moreno, Cherry Hill and others. Whenever we went out for location shooting, we were treated with a rock star reception.

We went to Batangas, just a few kilometres from Manila to performed at their fiesta. All of us stayed at the prominent politicians' houses. We performed live on stage with a dramatic act. I played a sad role and made the audience feel the emotion through my acting. Some even cried along with me. After the play we were surrounded with adoring fans. I felt so happy that I could connect well with the audience.

I ended up only attempting to perform in two movies from 1980 to 1982. *Mga Mata Ni Angelita* (The eyes of Angelita) was the name of the second movie I made. Julita Vega was the leading lady and I was her sister in the film. However, just before filming a tragedy happened at my house. My mum was cooking Lechon Kawali (deep fried pork) and the hot oil splashed on her face. We had to rush her to the hospital. Because of this harrowing incident I was not able to go to the film shooting, and I was replaced by Janice de Belen. I think the film had a bad omen, as the leading lady Julie de Vega soon after died in her sleep.

Never lose hope without fighting
Never give up without trying
Never stop loving, It's the reason for living
Never stop believing in yourself
It is the secret of success
Never stop trusting Him
He will always know
What Best for you

By Lorna Ramirez

CHAPTER 5:
BINONDO MANILA

After we left Greenhills we stayed at my other auntie's house in Binondo Manila. This district in Manila is known as *China Town*. It is the central of commerce and trade from all types of business, run by both Filipino and Chinese nationalities. My mum used her savings became a co-owner of my auntie's Karinderia (small take-away and eatery) so we could continue to support ourselves while living there.

We got lots of customers, mostly Chinese businessmen or jeepney and truck drivers. Our Karinderia was in front of Kami Plaza Hotel, a great location, well worth its rent. It was a good business and we had lots of customers to generate and a good income for both my auntie and mum!

My mum and I visited a friend in Project 4 where I met Christian, the son of my mum's friend. When I first met him I straight away had a crush on him. I felt like we connected with one another so easily. His family really liked me, however I lost interest in him because he was known to be a "ladies' man". On his graduation day, as per request of his parents I was the one to present him with his award medal. We remained friends until he finished his course in Criminology. We did not get in touch for many years after that, and I later learned that he had married and separated from his wife.

My brother was a sacristan (an altar boy) at our Binondo Parish Church. An altar boy is the one who assists the priest during the celebration of mass. We were all surprised and shocked to find my brother

CHAPTER 5: BINONDO MANILA

talking angrily at herself with no one around him and uttering words that we couldn't comprehend at a beach near our house. Once we found him, we took him home. He rested soundly for the night, and curiously the following day he had no recollection of the incident.

I had a distressing experience while I was in Manila; I was walking with my friend going to Divisoria (a commercial shop that sold low priced goods) at 5:00 am when suddenly some strange men approached us. The next thing I knew, the robbers were pointing a knife at my waist demanding money. I hit him hard and we ran away as fast as we could. After this experience, I began to really miss my life in Greenhills. It was peaceful and a safe suburb.

I was in Binondo Manila when Pope Paul VI visited the Philippines in 1071. I barely slept that night because I wanted to make sure I will be first in the line to greet him. It was a remarkable – one of the most memorable moments of my life. I was really lucky to be close to him and see him in person. Nothing could compare to the feeling of peace, contentment and serenity that I felt listening to his speech. His voice was so solemn and kind. He blessed all of us.

In our Binondo Parish Church an image or a statue of Sto Nino (child Jesus) is always kept on display, even until now. The Sto Nino is known for its miracle such as dancing feet, where many devotees have said to have witnessed the moving of Sto Nino feet as if he was dancing. I often went to this church so I might witness the miracle. Then one day when I was praying a strong fragrance of Jasmin flowers enveloped the whole church. I looked up and I saw the Sto Nino moving and dancing. It lasted only few seconds and I do not really know whether I was imagining only, but I fervently believed in my heart that I witnessed a miracle of the Sto Nino.

My Faith in God
With every quest I went through
With every trial I endured
With every frustration I had
With every fall I suffered
Without a doubt in my mind
I was able to go through all these
Because I knew that all these times
God would guide me and help me
Find The right way
And the right path to cross

***Excerpt from* My Innermost Thoughts**
by Lorna Ramirez

CHAPTER 6:
PAMPANGA

Pampanga is a province in the central Luzon region in the Philippines. This province is beside North Tarlac, and has Nueva Ecija to its northeast and Bulacan to its east. Our life in Binondo was taking shape and our Karinderia was doing well, however after couple of years my older sister Ate Narcisa was about to get married to a man from the Pampanga province. Our family then decided to relocate to Pampanga along with my Kuya Tony, so we could be close to my Ate Narcisa to support her.

Ate Narcisa had a grand wedding in Pampanga, attended by friends and families from both sides. In Pampanga I worked to assist a family for a few months. The American husband was so kind and yet the Filipina wife was taking advantage of his kindness and generosity by having an affair. It sickened me so after only few months working with the family I resigned.

In Pampanga I also helped my Ate Narcisa financially, especially with all her troubles and miseries in life. Her husband had been unfaithful to her, but she managed to pull through and was able to raise and look after her five children - all boys.

For a while we rented an apartment, then I started my own business selling street food. I sold barbecue, hot dogs, and banana cue. My street food business was a success and I started saving with the intentions of buying my own house for my family. With enough money saved I started to own and invest in a Sari-Sari Store (milk bar as commonly called in Australia). My business was booming. At this stage I also expanded to include take-away foods. My store was located in a strategic position, in front of Clark Airbase (This was formerly a United States Military Facility, managed by the United States Airforce).

I had a good income and was able to save enough to buy a two-storey house. When we were financially stable in Pampanga some of my brothers and sisters joined us; Rowena, Patricio, and Cerella. My Dad decided to stay in Leyte, but he eventually became so lonely, and without my mum. he often turned to alcohol to drown his sorrows.

By the age of 20, I owned a successful business and really felt that all my sacrifices were worthwhile and very rewarding. At this age I met my first love. A good looking American Pilot. We were both shy and my family was so strict that we did not have the time to get to know each other that well. We were not able to go out on a date. Many of my friends were dissuading me from him and encouraging me to end up the relationship. Some of them even went to say that pilots are unfaithful and have plenty of relationships at every destination they go to.

Though it hurt I decided to end the affair. I had no

choice as I was providing for both my mum and my siblings. Our relationship only lasted one year Yes, it was the best thing to do as I have so many plans for the future, but it was hard nonetheless. My sorrow and longing for him was alleviated after time, and because I had so many friends who showed support by taking me out to movies, restaurants, and the disco. I ended up having a fun time with my close friends and without them I wouldn't have known what to do!

Having a successful business entailed a lot of work and there were so many sacrifices that I had to make. Nevertheless, I was so happy that I had worked hard to finally fulfil my dreams of having a house and a successful business of my own.

SPECIAL MOMENTS

Each special moment
Has that special meaning
That will be forever
Embedded in our hearts
Each challenge and endeavour
We have gone through
Needs patience, hope and perseverance
From each failure and mistake we have made
Lessons can be learned
Can be used as an inspiration
To start all over again
Till we have reached our dreams

***Excerpt from* My Innermost Thoughts**
By Lorna Ramirez

CHAPTER 7: MY SOULMATE

My relationship with the pilot had ended, so I concentrated and focused more on my business. After few months I met Barry Mill, a tourist from Australia. He was a tanker driver in Australia, and he was twenty years older than me. We connected and bonded straight away. I was impressed with his honesty and his mild mannered behaviour.

With honesty when we first started seeing each other he told me that he had a Filipina fiancée here in the Philippines, and they were about to get married.

He financially supported her family and supported her Secretarial course here. He was so frustrated and shocked to found out that her fiancée at the same time had an intimate relationship with a younger American guy. He soon ended the relationship.

Barry showed me documents detailing their wedding plans and without hesitation he ripped the documents in front of me. His fiancée tried so hard to reconcile with him, but Barry refused to take her back again.

One sunny afternoon he said, "Elvira I have to go back to Australia next week, but I will be back after six months to propose. Blushing I said, "Barry I will decide once you come back. Only time will tell if we are meant for each other". He assured me that he would surely come back.

Months passed and Barry and I had no communication, so I thought he had forgotten his promise. I continue to concentrate and worked hard in expanding my business. I had almost forgotten Barry when one day to my surprise he visited and came to Pampanga to propose. With a smile and with a joyous tone in his voice he asked, "Elvira will you marry me?" While showing a beautiful engagement ring. I was so flattered, and I trusted him and within my heart I know he was sincere and honest. I said yes.

He did the right thing by talking to my family about his intention to marry me. My mum was adamant at first, and she said to me "Elvira are you sure you are making the right decision, and remember he is older than you by twenty years can you deal with that?" I replied and said" Do not worry mum I have made my decision, and this is what I want. Within my heart I know he is good man and I believe I will be happy with him. My mum and family supported and respected my decision.

We were married on August 12, 1985 at the Church of Christ Angeles City and the reception was held at one of the finest restaurants in Angeles City.

FINDING LOVE

Being in love we start
To rediscover our inner self
And the real meaning
Of What life is all about
Finding love is magical
Moments and precious time
We shared with someone
We truly love and adore
Finding love is priceless

***Excerpt from* Reflective Contemplations**
By Lorna Ramirez

CHAPTER 8: AUSTRALIA

I finally married my soul mate Barry Mills. He was 20 years older than me, however deep down I knew he was a good man, with a big heart, kind and gentle. After few months he went back to Australia and told me to follow up with the application he had submitted to the Australian Embassy showing that I am his legal wife and will be applying for visa for a permanent residency in Australia to be reunited with him.

My oldest son was conceived in the Philippines.

It was quite a challenge preparing all the documents Especially since I was heavily pregnant at that time. I migrated to Australia on March 11, 1986. I was ecstatic, though I found it hard to leave my family behind. It was a cultural shock upon arriving in Australia. I had to adjust for several months to the Australian lifestyle. Nevertheless, I was so grateful and lucky that Barry and his two children accepted and welcomed me with open arms. They treated me like a princess. Without exaggeration, my stepson insisted that he would peel apples for me, and my stepdaughter would often go to Victoria market to buy seafood for me. They knew I didn't eat lamb or veal and they were accommodating to that. My husband Barry would buy Chinese food just for me. As time went by, I slowly adapted to my new environment.

Even though I was showered with love and attention by Barry and his family I was still lonely and homesick, really missing my mum, and my brothers and sisters. I started making new friends here in Australia and this really helped to alleviate my loneliness. Some of my friends that I met down the track were also Filipina wives of Barry's friends who came to Australia a few years after me.

With the help of my friends, I started to appreciate the Australian's way of life. We often went out together with our husbands to see movies, dining in nice restaurants, attending concerts, and visiting beautiful places in Melbourne. My husband Barry is a good provider and he worked hard for his family.

When I decided to migrate to Australia, I left my business of Sari Sari store and karinderia to my siblings. I had a dream of expanding my business even though I was here in Australia, but to my disappointment they were not interested and mismanaged my businesses. The businesses were then sold when our youngest sister had a domestic problem with her husband. Her husband had an affair with a girl working in a bar, and when her and her husband separated, she fought to keep her child, thus costing her a lot of money for a lawyer and court proceedings.

In spite of having so many friends in Australia I really missed my mum. Barry was aware of that, so he sponsored my mum to come to Australia. I was truly happy that at last I would be reunited with her. At last I would have someone to talk to who truly understands me. My husband was busy working, and as a truck driver he was always on the road, but even when he was home he didn't talk much.

After I had settled in Australia and had my first child, I had the chance to work at the Langham Hotel. My boss liked my performance and all my workmates were all friendly. Then I had my second pregnancy. A very difficult journey for me. I was vomiting and feeling nauseated all the time and could hardly eat and my weight plummeted so severely that I had no choice but to resign from my work. However, since I had a good track work record, my supervisor assured me that I could go back and work after my maternity leave. I was so lucky that mum was with me and looked after me throughout my pregnancy.

When our children were young our family often went to NSW Merimbula for a month or two for a holiday. Merimbula is a beautiful place in New South Wales. They have beautiful beaches, shops and restaurants. It was a haven for tourists, the heart of the Sapphire coast. Indeed it was our favourite destination for our holiday.

In the year 1991 on June 15th, there was a volcanic eruption that affected the densely populated area near the Mount Pinatubo in the Philippines. Giant mudflows of very hot ashes with high speed avalanches flowed through hundreds of miles to the residential areas. It damaged property after property and killed hundreds of people living in the area. My house there was totally covered with ash because of the eruption. From Australia I prayed for the safety of my brothers and sisters. I was so relieved to learn they were not hurt during the eruption. I managed to get that house fixed up and sold, and with the profits I financed youngest sister's airfare for her immigration to the United States of America. She is now happy living there with a family there.

In Australia I became a care worker in a nursing home, and I have been working there until present. It is a very demanding job. With three children and my mum who got sick in Australia I spent most of my time just for my family. My mum was sick for two years, so I did everything in spite of my demanding job. I did all the groceries, the cooking, and dropping and picking up my kids from school. At times I needed help from my friends to pick up the kids from school.

When she first came, my mum suffered a few strokes and she was admitted to hospital several times during her early years in Australia. I really miss my mum. Unfortunately, she passed away ten years ago with a pneumonia complication. One of my brothers visited her here in Australia when she was very sick. None of my sisters and brothers migrated to Australia. They were happy and already successful in the Philippines.

FEAR OF THE UNKNOWN

Fear of the unknown is one of the reasons
We are reluctant to do the things
Out of our comfort zone
But once we have decided to take the risk
And have succeeded, the benefits are endless
Hence, we will never look back
For those of us who have failed
At least we can learn from our mistakes
Thus inspiring us to do better next time around

***Excerpt from* My Innermost Thoughts**
by Lorna Ramirez

CHAPTER 9:
MY HUSBAND BARRY MILLS

My husband was very supportive and loving person. I liked him the first time I met him in the Philippines. He had good sense of humour, a kind heart and was a good provider to his family. He loved my family and agreed to sponsor my mother to come here to. He loved sport, music, and drinking his beer with his friends. Before I met my husband, he was married and divorced and had 2 sons from his first wife. Even before we married, he had several health issues, such as severe gout, and at times he spent hours staying in bed wrought with pain. He suffered from high blood pressure and high cholesterol due to an unhealthy diet and lack of exercise. He didn't drink water only beer. He loved his meats and rich sweet foods. As a tanker driver from Caltex, he was on the road all the time eating junk food, with no exercise, thus putting on more weight in the past years.

Eight years ago, Barry had a heart operation. He survived and lead a normal life. When our kids were young, we used to go out as family but lately, as my kids were now grown up, he preferred to stay home and drink beer with our neighbour. At the age of 65 he retired, and with so much time on his hands he became inactive, just watching TV and drinking beer; a recipe for disaster. Tragically, he passed away at the age of 78. On the 16th of April 2018 he was watching TV in the lounge room just like any other day, when he fell asleep and suffered from a devastating heart attack that ended his life. As his wish, he was cremated at the Altona Cemetery.

Chapter 9: MY HUSBAND BARRY MILLS

We raised three sons together. Our eldest Darren is married and works as a business manager for Sports Australia and for the AFL (Australia Football League). My second son David runs his own business as a Plasterer. My youngest son Grant still lives with me, and is studying a course in IT. I will always love Barry, and he will be in my heart forever. We had wonderful memories together and he would do everything to make me happy. Rest in peace my dear until one day we will be reunited in heaven.

A SONG OF LOVE

I can not count the number
Of the stars in the sky
But I can see its brightness
Beauty and grandeur
I can not fathom the depth
Of the deep blue sea
But I can feel its serenity
Calmness and tranquillity
It is the same as
I can not tell you
How much I love you
But I can feel within my heart
The depth and the intensity
Of my love for you

***Excerpt from* Reflective Contemplations**
By Lorna Ramirez

CHAPTER 10: MOVING ON, LIFE WITHOUT BARRY

It is still hurts to live without Barry, but I have to be strong for my kids. There are moments that I felt my life was empty, and I prayed hard to overcome loneliness in my heart and soul. I was so blessed and lucky to be surrounded with loving family and friends. At the least, it alleviated my aching heart and help me grieve my dear Barry.

Together my friends and I would always go to functions and parties, eating out, or just having girls' fun. I am so lucky and blessed to still have a job. With my job as a carer in a nursing home, I feel happy especially since I feel like I have a special bond with my patients. I love to look after them, and give them special care. My heart bleeds that at times the relatives of my patients have forgotten to visit their loved ones at the nursing home.

I attended several Filipino Organisations and met some new friends in the past few years. I am also a dancer in a Filipino original dance group. We were even invited to some events to showcase our dancing.

However sometimes your kindness can be abused. A friend of mine borrowed $800 and never re-paid me. I was so frustrated considering that my husband had just died and I need the money. I tried to get in touch with her, but it remains futile, I cannot find nor locate her whereabouts. I prayed to God. After few months since Barry had passed away, I was struggling to deal the situation. I really missed him. On the other hand I was to blessed I have three wonderful children who were always there for me.

ODE TO THE LOST LOVED ONE

Happiness and life together

We once had

Has been taken away from us

All those that we shared

Those precious moments

And precious time that we had

It's now just past memories

It's all that I have

They say time will heal

The pain I feel

But the scar and loneliness

In my heart

Will always be there

That will never take time to heal

Excerpt from **My Passion My Calling**
By Lorna Ramirez

CHAPTER 11:
MIRACLES

Do you believe in Miracles? I do. This chapter is solely for all the miracles I have had in my life. My most memorable miracle was when I had a second life. at the age of one year old I had a food poisoning episode. My mum said I was so dehydrated, and that I lost my pulse for a few minutes. I stopped breathing. The herbal doctor in our village did not give up and continued to give me lots of herbs in a traditional concoction. I couldn't be transferred to a hospital as it would take too many hours to reach the town. It was raining so heavily that the roads and bridges were impassable. Mum and dad prayed and prayed, begging for a miracle to happen. I slowly regained my pulse and was alive again. All my family hugged at what a joyous moment for us.

At that time that my husband Barry had his heart operation, I could not be at his side as I had a commitment in Bendigo. I prayed and prayed for his wellbeing from so far away. All I could do was pray for him in the church. I cried, and as tears flowed from my face I prayed to the Mother Mary statue, begging her to save my Barry. Suddenly I heard a voice coming from nowhere that said "It is okay my child, he will recover." I had goose bumps but despite the shock I overjoyed and I knew that my prayers were heard. After few hours my son rang up to say that Barry had a successful operation.

MIRACLE AT THE HOSPITAL

The doctor at the hospital informed that my mum's heartbeat had stopped for few seconds, hence she was placed in an artificial heart machine. I started praying to God and said, "Please Jesus, save my mum." I was sitting at my mum's bedside when suddenly I felt a spark on my body starting from my toes and spreading to the top of my head. My mum called out to me saying desperately "Who are you?" I replied franticly, "It's me Elvira your daughter." She smiled to me and said, "I had a wonderful dream with beautiful rows of flowers and angels singing." I then hugged my mum and called the doctor. It's a miracle my mum had awaken from an induced coma. I knelt prayed and thanking God that my mum was alive.

THIRD EYE

This is called also mind's eye or inner eye. it is a spiritual mindset, especially for when you are doing meditation or intensive prayer. Sometimes when your third eye opens you can receive messages from God and see spirits and things that ordinary human beings can't see. You can see through the beyond and begin to utilise psychic powers. When I was growing up in our barrio, I witnessed an old lady turning into a pig, and a few times I saw a big basin at the top of a tree shining with light that was so impossibly bright.

GLITTERS ON MY HANDS (ESCARCHAS)

Escarchas is an unexplained phenomenon, it is the appearance of gold dust to one's hands, faces and bodies. This is prominent in some Catholic and Protestant circles. Only a few are lucky to experience this phenomenon This miracle usually appears in deep and fervent prayers and atmospheres. This is one of the many miracles that most people will be sceptical of. This golden filter coating appears like sparkling diamonds. It is indeed a phenomenon that no one can explain and is sometimes called Gods Glitter. I am one of the lucky few who had experienced this wonderful and blissful feeling of Escarchas.

Sister Emma is our holy lady, a God's helper. She was the one who brought the statue of Virgin Mary to Australia. Sister Emma lives in Canada and she is able to communicate with God in her backyard surrounded with trees.

In a friend's house where she, brought the statue of Mother Mary on August 2016, we were praying with deep devotion. My prayers were so intense and suddenly I saw my hands and arms covered with gold dust. I continue my prayers and I started crying with joy and happiness, I am sure that I was blessed having this miracle.

I was still in awe, and could not believe the miracle, so I went to the church and talked to our parish priest about the appearance of glitter. However the priest was adamant in not believing my story and jokingly said "I can loan you to the Pawn shop since you're made of gold." I did not say a word. I was hurt that even some of my friends had doubts and do not believe. I had the glitter experience a few times, and it has now been more than a year since I have experienced the said miracle. Regardless what everybody said, I believe in my heart and soul that this is not a fraud or fake. In my mind I still believe that God loves me so much, hence giving this blessed miracle.

Healing Power

The son of one of my friends was seriously sick at the hospital. He was in an induced coma, sleeping for almost a week. My friend took me to the hospital, asking me to pray for her son who was seriously sick. I gladly obliged. At the hospital I prayed with such intensity for almost thirty minutes. I touched his head and asked God to give this young man a chance to live. Glitters appeared on my hands. I did not say anything to my friend. After few minutes

my friend took me to the cafeteria to have a cup of coffee. I consoled my friend and said "Do not worry, we have to accept God's will." We went back to the room and found nurses and a doctor attending to her son. With a smile on their faces they said, "He has awaken." Tears of joy and happiness were felt by my friend and she hugged me and said, "Thank you Elvira for your prayers." That was one moment in my life I will never forget. God is good.

Miracle at the Highway Makati Philippines

I often visited my cousins in Makati, and every time I visited them they always reminded and warned me not to cross the highway near their place because it was known for pedestrian and truck accidents. Despite of all their concern I did exactly the opposite. One night I was crossing the highway, I saw a big truck coming my way, the truck's light was so bright it almost blinded me, I thought I was going to die. I felt a strong wind behind my back, and I passed out.

When I woke up, I was on the other side of the road. I pinched myself in disbelief. I was still alive, breathing. There were so many questions in my mind that I need answers. Who pushed me at that moment? Why? Well without any doubt, I believe I was saved by my guardian angel. I realised people won't believe and be sceptical of what I said but my strong faith in God will always be in my heart.

This is my story and I am proud to be someone who will always believe in miracles. No matter what people will say, I am absolutely sure that I am one of the blessed few who have experienced the miracles of life. My undying love of God will be always treasured and kept in my heart. His love will always guide me and protect me as I walk through my journey of life. Amen.

MIRACLES

Who said miracles do not exist anymore?
From the moment I open my eyes each morning
I see the sun shining in the sky
Or hear the sound of the rain
Pouring down on my roof
I see life in it
Beautiful creations from God
Enjoying the sun
Feasting from the pouring rain, the crops that we planted
Bearing its fruit
I see miracles in these
Indeed, about the harmonious relationship
Of nature and mankind
A simple thing I can say is
"Miracle of life"

**Excerpt from My Innermost Thoughts
By Lorna Ramirez**

CHAPTER 12:
FAMILY PHOTOS

I was in my teens and with my best friend in the Philippines

Barry my late husband and my oldest son Darren

CHAPTER 12: FAMILY PHOTOS

My Mum with my family

My beautiful Mum and me

With my beloved husband Barry

*My beautiful loving family:
Late husband Barry, Darren, David and Grant*

CHAPTER 12: FAMILY PHOTOS

With my 2 young sons, Darren and David

Having fun with my friends and me in the Philippines

With my son

*My children,
David and Darren*

More fun with friends and mum

CHAPTER 12: FAMILY PHOTOS

*another friend of mine in Australia
at an event we attended*

My photo at the age of 35

A younger photo of myself

My mom(Mum) and my three boys

CHAPTER 12: FAMILY PHOTOS

Young Darren

My young gorgeous two sons

My late husband Barry's family

This is a Jeepney, a form of transportation in the Philippines. My Family inside the Jeepney

my youngest son, Grant and me at a Gold Coast restaurant

BOOKS BY
LORNA RAMIREZ

This book was written by Lorna Ramirez to reach those people who need encouragement, enlightenment and strength when facing adversities and predicaments in life. The author is a keen observer of human behaviour and emotions, and wants to share with readers young and old from all walks of life her thoughts about life in general, to encourage self-motivation, positive attitude, and believing in yourself.

Lorna Ramirez wrote this book so she could share her wisdoms with others. She has been an observer of human behaviour and emotions and has built up her own personal philosophies throughout her life. This book is a collection of her strong beliefs and convictions and offers encouragement and enlightenment to others who may be lost and confused or be looking for some positive advice and assistance. Lorna Ramirez is a woman of strong beliefs in her faith and advocates believing in oneself, perseverance when times are difficult and living in the present.

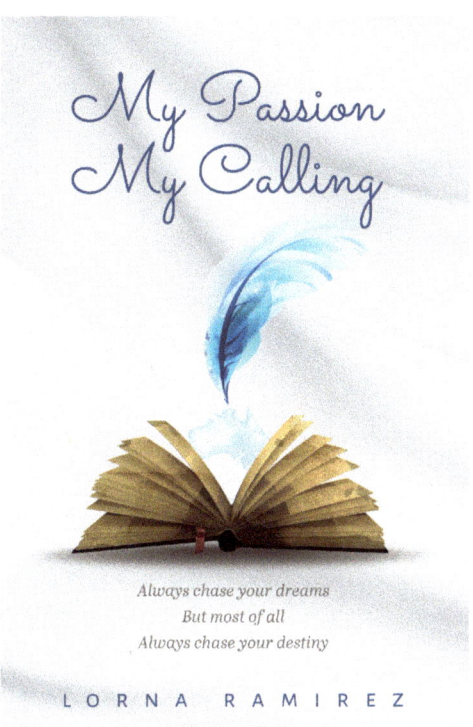

This authentic story about a Filipino migrant family settling in Melbourne in 1977 is a fascinating read, as it tells of the emotions, the ups and downs, the government assistance in those days, the practicalities, the difficulties, the sudden change of lifestyle and culture but also the joys of living in Australia in the 1970s, a 'paradise' in so many ways, with great opportunities for a good life.

The wife suddenly is confronted with severe trauma, closely followed by another, a time in their lives when everything appeared perfect. Her near death experience results in new beliefs and understanding and inspires her to write.

After a traumatic experience at the hands of four men, Eliza Martinez leaves her family and home in the Philippines to find happiness in Australia. But tragedy happens again in her life. Again she must overcome all predicaments in order to pull through and move on.

As a twist of fate makes her a victim of love, she realises the importance of having support during her journey through life. She comes to rely on her friends and family — even as she considers what it would mean to start a family of her own.

This is a story of romance, forbidden love and courage; a story of human sufferings, vulnerability and how the choices we make change our lives.

This book was written by Lorna Ramirez to reach those people who need encouragement, enlightenment and strength when facing adversities and predicaments in life. The author is a keen observer of human behaviour and emotions, and wants to share with readers young and old from all walks of life her thoughts about life in general, to encourage self-motivation, positive attitude, and believing in yourself.

With all Lorna's books and written articles in Melbourne, she has always spread and promoted the advocacy of Love, Acceptance, and Tolerance regardless of creed, race, gender and beliefs.

www.ingramcontent.com/pod-product-compliance
Lightning Source LLC
Chambersburg PA
CBHW040554010526
44110CB00054B/2679